7600

D1061591

Army

DELTA FORCE

by Carlos Alvarez

TORQUE
TM

BELLWETHER MEDIA ★ MINNEAPOLIS, MN

Library of Congress
Alvarez, Carlos, 1968–
  Army Delta Force / by Carlos Alvarez.
      p. cm. — (Torque: Armed forces)
  Summary: "Amazing photography accompanies engaging information about the Army Delta Force. The combination of high-interest subject matter and light text is intended for students in grades 3 through 7"—Provided by publisher.
  Includes bibliographical references and index.
  ISBN 978-1-60014-290-1 (hardcover : alk. paper)
  1. United States. Army. Delta Force—Juvenile literature. I. Title.
  UA34.S64A48 2010
  356'.167—dc22   2009008494

030110   1160

CONTENTS

★ ★ ★

★ ★ ★

Chapter One
WHAT IS DELTA FORCE?

The United States Army's Delta Force specializes in **covert operations**. It is the most secret group in the U.S. military. Delta Force is also known as Special Forces Operational Detachment-Delta.

Delta Force missions include **counterterrorism** and **hostage** rescue. Deltas also perform other missions that need quick and deadly action. Delta Force and its missions are top secret. The government even denied that Delta Force existed for many years.

Chapter Two
WEAPONS AND GEAR

Deltas use a wide range of weapons. Many Deltas carry the M4 **carbine**. They also use submachine guns such as the MP5. Sniper rifles such as the M14 can take out targets from long distances. Deltas are also trained to use heavy weapons and explosives.

M4 carbine

Deltas often carry weapons from the region they are assigned. For example, the Russian-made AK-47 is often carried because it is used all around the world.

AK-47

Deltas often work undercover. They need to blend in with a crowd. They dress in street clothes. They speak foreign languages. Even their vehicles are disguised as normal civilian vehicles.

Night-vision goggles

Deltas need a variety of other gear. Deltas know what kind of gear each mission will require. **Global positioning systems (GPS)** help them find their way to specific locations. **Night-vision goggles** help them see at night. **SCUBA gear** allows them to breathe while underwater. This equipment helps them complete missions in many environments.

Chapter Three

LIFE IN DELTA FORCE

Delta Force is based out of Fort Bragg, North Carolina, along with the Green Berets.

Deltas come from all four branches of the military. Most Deltas come from the **Green Berets** and the **Army Rangers**. These soldiers are highly trained before they join Delta Force.

Delta Force recruits go through a tough selection process. Recruits need special skills. They need the ability to speak several languages. They also need excellent **marksmanship**. Selected recruits go through a six-month training program. It includes intense physical training. This includes a 40-mile (64-kilometer) hike carrying heavy equipment. Recruits must be able to **navigate** in unfamiliar places. They also go through physical and mental tests.

Colonel Charles Beckwith created Delta Force in October of 1977. Beckwith based the Deltas on a similar British force called the British Special Air Service.

Recruits who complete the training join a **squadron**. Most new Deltas go into combat squadrons. Others go into specialized groups such as **aviation** and **intelligence**.

Within squadrons are smaller groups called **troops**. Each troop includes twelve Deltas. Troops can be further divided into mission teams. A mission team can be as small as one member.

Life in Delta Force is filled with hard work, dedication, and secrecy. Few have what it takes to join this elite group. Those who do serve have a unique way to protect their country.

Deltas can grow long hair and beards to help them blend in with civilians.

GLOSSARY

* * *

Army Rangers—the special ground forces of the United States Army

aviation—to do with flight

carbine—a short-barreled repeating rifle

counterterrorism—a military mission designed to discover or prevent terrorist activity

covert operation—a top secret mission

global positioning system (GPS)—a device that uses satellites orbiting Earth to determine a precise position on the globe

Green Berets—a name for the U.S. Army Special Forces, a group of highly trained soldiers

hostage—a person held captive by a criminal or terrorist group as a means of getting something

intelligence—the group of Deltas responsible for gathering information on enemies

marksmanship—the ability to accurately fire a rifle over long distances

navigate—to find one's way in unfamiliar terrain

night-vision goggles—a special set of glasses that allow the wearer to see at night

SCUBA gear—a self-contained, underwater breathing apparatus; SCUBA gear provides divers with oxygen to breathe while underwater.

squadron—a large team of soldiers who work together to perform missions

troop—a division within a squadron; in Delta Force, a troop includes 12 Deltas.

TO LEARN MORE

★ ★ ★

AT THE LIBRARY

David, Jack. *Green Berets*. Minneapolis, Minn.: Bellwether, 2009.

David, Jack. *United States Army*. Minneapolis, Minn.: Bellwether, 2008.

Riley, Gail Blasser. *Delta Force in Action*. New York, N.Y.: Bearport, 2008.

ON THE WEB

Learning more about the Delta Force is as easy as 1, 2, 3.

1. Go to www.factsurfer.com.

2. Enter "Delta Force" into the search box.

3. Click the "Surf" button and you will see a list of related Web sites.

With factsurfer.com, finding more information is just a click away.

INDEX

★ ★ ★

The images in this book are reproduced through the courtesy of the United States Department of Defense.